How
Your Body
Works

What Happens
When You

Breathe?

Jacqui Bailey

PowerKiDS
press.

New York

Published in 2009 by The Rosen Publishing Group Inc.
29 East 21st Street, New York, NY 10010

First Edition

Senior Editor: Jennifer Schofield
Consultant: Dr Patricia Macnair
Designer: Phipps Design
Illustrator: Ian Thompson
Picture Researcher: Kathy Lockley
Proofreader: Susie Brooks

Library of Congress Cataloging-in-Publication Data

Bailey, Jacqui.
  What happens when you breathe? / Jacqui Bailey. — 1st ed.
    p. cm. — (How your body works)
  Includes index.
  ISBN 978-1-4042-4428-3 (library binding)
  ISBN 978-1-4358-2618-2 (paperback)
  ISBN 978-1-4358-2632-8 (6-pack)
  1. Respiration—Juvenile literature. I. Title.
  QP121.B184 2008
  612.2'2—dc22

                                          2007041764

Manufactured in China

Picture acknowledgements
Cory Bevington/Photofusion: 25; John Birdsall Social Issues Library: 20, 22;
Bromberger-Hoover/Jupiterimages: 6; David R. Frazier Photolibrary Inc/
Alamy Images: Cover, 17; Tony Freeman/Art Directors Photo Library: 15TL;
Ingolf Hatz/zefa/Corbis: 14; Image Quest Marine/Alamy Images: 9; Andrew
Lambert/Art Directors Photo Library: 27; NASA: 19; Jake Norton/Alamy Images:
18; Bill Robbins/Jupiterimages: 21; Robert Thompson/NHPA: 15BR; Cathrine
Wessel/Corbis: 26; Watts/Wayland Archive: 7,8,13,

Contents

Why do we breathe?

We breathe to stay alive. When we breathe, we take air into our bodies. Air contains a gas called oxygen. We need oxygen to have energy.

Without energy, our bodies would stop working and we would die very quickly—within a few minutes. We use energy when we are active, but we also need it for lots of other things. In fact, everything our bodies do uses energy.

We use energy to keep ourselves warm and to cool down when we are too hot. We use it to grow, to heal parts of ourselves when we get hurt, and to fight illnesses. We use energy when we eat, drink, talk, think, and even when we sleep.

We start breathing when we are born and do not stop until we die. Over 70 years, a person will breathe in and out more than 500 million times.

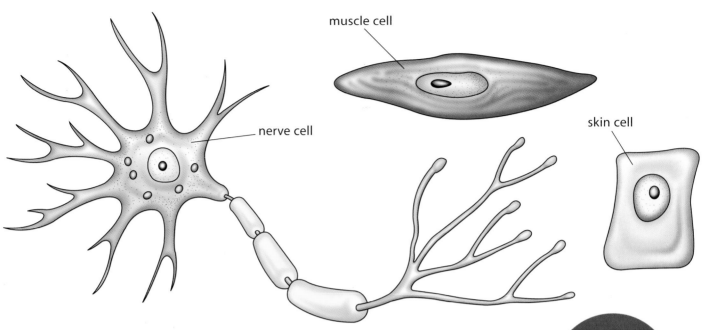

muscle cell

nerve cell

skin cell

These are some of the cell types we have in our body. In real life, these cells can be seen only through a microscope.

Our bodies are made out of billions of tiny things called cells. There are muscle cells, skin cells, bone cells, nerve cells, and lots more. Each cell has a job to do and it needs energy to do it. Without the oxygen we breathe, our cells would have no energy.

See for yourself

How often do you breathe?

Sit still and listen to your breathing. How many times do you breathe in and out in one minute? Use a stopwatch to time yourself—one breath in and one breath out count as one full breath. When people are sitting still or resting, they take about 12 to 15 full breaths every minute.

Breathing in

You breathe in through your nose or mouth. Air travels down your throat, through a tube called the windpipe, and into your lungs.

Your lungs are inside your chest. You have two of them, one on each side. They are soft and squishy like a sponge. Your lungs are surrounded by rows of bones called ribs. You can feel your ribs when you put your hands on the sides of your chest.

The ribs are held in place by muscles. When you breathe in, these muscles tighten and pull your ribs upward and outward. This makes more space in your chest so that air can be pulled into the lungs. When you breathe out, the rib muscles relax. The ribs sink down and in, making the space in your chest smaller again. This squeezes used-up air out of your lungs.

We cannot breathe under water. Swimmers learn to lift their nose and mouth out of the water to take in air.

Another muscle also helps you to breathe in and out. It is called the diaphragm. The diaphragm sits underneath the lungs and ribs. It is like a thick, rubbery shelf that separates your chest from the lower part of your body. It tightens and becomes flatter when you breathe in, and relaxes and bulges upward as you breathe out.

How many ribs?

Your ribs are joined to a bone that runs down the middle of your back, called a backbone. All animals with a backbone have ribs. Humans have 12 pairs of ribs, but a snake may have more than 200 pairs.

These are the parts your body uses to breathe air in and out.

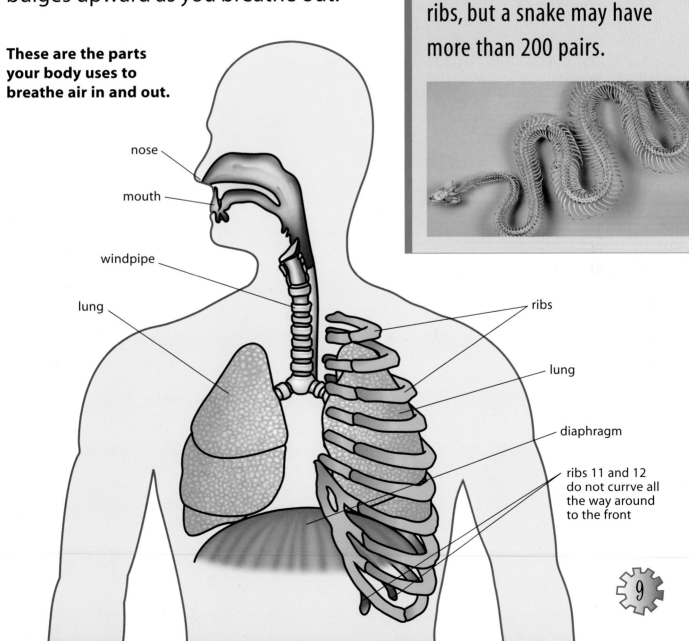

nose

mouth

windpipe

lung

ribs

lung

diaphragm

ribs 11 and 12 do not currve all the way around to the front

Inside your lungs

On the outside, your lungs are smooth and slippery. This helps them to slide against the ribs and muscles in your chest as they fill with air. Inside, they are packed with millions of tubes.

Just before the windpipe reaches the lungs, it splits into two branches. The right branch goes into the right lung and the left branch into the left lung. These two branches are called bronchi. Inside the lungs, the bronchi split again and again into smaller and smaller tubes, spreading out like the branches of an upside-down tree.

The smallest tubes are called bronchioles. At the end of each bronchiole is a little bunch of round, hollow balls.

The wrong way!

When you swallow something "the wrong way," it gets into your windpipe instead of going down the tube that leads to your stomach. Small pieces of food can be coughed up to clear them from your windpipe, but a large blockage can stop you from breathing.

The balls are tiny air sacs called alveoli. They are so small, you would need about 40 of them to measure about $\frac{1}{25}$ inch (one millimeter).

The walls of the alveoli are incredibly thin—so thin, in fact, that gases can pass through them. This is where the oxygen that you breathe in passes into the rest of your body.

Each of your lungs is filled with lots of tiny tubes, ending in bunches of bubble-shaped alveoli.

food tube leading to stomach

bronchiole

windpipe

bronchi

bronchioles

lung

alveoli

lung

From lungs to heart

Oxygen cannot travel around your body on its own. It needs to be carried by something. This is one of the jobs your blood does.

Your blood travels around your body through a system of tubes called blood vessels. Blood vessels reach into every part of your body, including your lungs. Like your breathing tubes, blood vessels are quite large in the center of your body, but become narrower and narrower as they branch out.

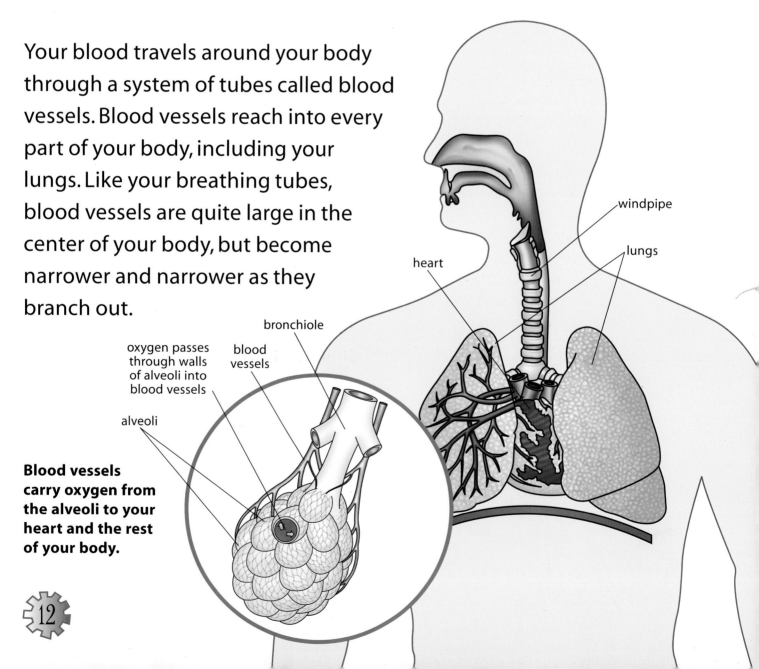

oxygen passes through walls of alveoli into blood vessels

bronchiole

blood vessels

alveoli

windpipe

lungs

heart

Blood vessels carry oxygen from the alveoli to your heart and the rest of your body.

Tiny blood vessels wrap around each alveolus (alveolus is the singular of alveoli). When you breathe in, oxygen passes through the thin walls of the alveoli into these blood vessels, and is soaked up by the blood. The blood vessels in your lungs lead straight to your heart, and the oxygen is carried out of the lungs and into the heart.

The heart is a muscle that works like a pump. It squeezes and relaxes with a regular rhythm called a heartbeat. Every time your heart beats, it pushes blood around your body. The oxygen-rich blood arrives in the left side of your heart, and from here it is sent to all the other parts of your body.

See for yourself

Blue blood

You can see blood vessels on the inside of your wrist, just underneath your skin. Blood is red, but the vessels look like thin blue lines. This is partly because you are seeing them through your skin, and partly because the blood in these vessels does not have much oxygen. This makes the blood darker.

Oxygen for energy

As blood flows around your body, oxygen is taken out of it along the way. Every tiny cell in your body uses oxygen for energy.

Energy is stored in the food we eat. We need energy to keep our bodies going, just as a car engine needs gasoline. When you eat, your body breaks down the food into tiny pieces. The pieces are then sent to your blood to be carried around your body.

A lot of the food we eat contains a type of sugar called glucose. When the cells in your body need energy, they take oxygen and glucose from your blood and mix them together. Mixing oxygen and glucose releases the energy stored in the glucose. At the same time, the glucose and oxygen are changed into water and a gas called carbon dioxide.

Most of our energy comes from the glucose in food. Foods such as pasta contain a lot of glucose.

14

When you exercise and get too hot, your body uses some of its unwanted water as sweat to cool you down.

The cells use the released energy to do their work, such as making muscles move or growing new cells. Some of the water is used, too. Any unused water is treated as waste and sent out of your body. Carbon dioxide is also treated as waste—your body uses your lungs to get rid of it.

Air holes

Almost all animals use oxygen for energy. They do not all get their oxygen in the same way, though. For example, insects do not have lungs. Instead, they have little holes all over their bodies that let in air. The holes lead to tubes that carry the air around inside their bodies.

Breathing out

Every time you breathe out, your body gets rid of unwanted gases and water.

As blood travels around your body delivering food and oxygen, it collects unused water and carbon dioxide, and carries them back to the heart. The heart pumps them along blood vessels to the alveoli, where they pass from the blood into the lungs. When you breathe out, the carbon dioxide and water are pushed up the windpipe and out of your nose or mouth, along with any unused oxygen.

Inside your lungs, the alveoli collect carbon dioxide and waste water from your blood and put oxygen into your blood.

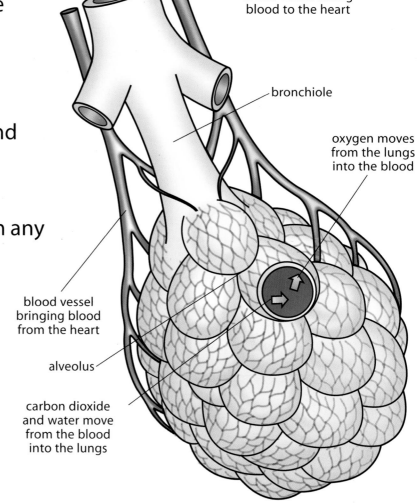

blood vessel taking blood to the heart

bronchiole

oxygen moves from the lungs into the blood

blood vessel bringing blood from the heart

alveolus

carbon dioxide and water move from the blood into the lungs

The air you breathe out has been warmed up by your body. The warmth turns the water in your breath into tiny droplets called water vapor. You cannot usually see your breath, but when the air around you is cold, it turns the water vapor to mist—making your breath look like smoke.

Carbon dioxide is bad for our bodies, which is why we need to get rid of it. But green plants need carbon dioxide to live. They mix it with water to make food. When they do this, they give off a waste gas just like we do. This waste gas is oxygen. Without green plants, there would be no oxygen for us to breathe.

When you breathe out on a cold day, the waste water in your breath looks like smoky mist.

See for yourself

Watching your breath

Put a small mirror in the fridge for about 15 minutes. Wipe it clean, then hold it close to your mouth and breathe on it. When the tiny water droplets in your warm breath hit the cold surface of the mirror, they turn into bigger droplets that you see as mist.

What is air?

Air is a mixture of things. It is made up mainly of oxygen, water, and carbon dioxide. There are other gases in it, too, as well as tiny pieces of dust and other particles that are so small we need a microscope to see them.

Air wraps around the Earth like an invisible skin. As you move away from the Earth's surface, the air gets thinner and thinner, and there is less and less oxygen in it. In space there is no air at all.

Not having enough oxygen to breathe makes us sick and can kill us. People who climb very high mountains take extra oxygen with them.

Air is very special to the Earth. It protects us from the burning heat of the Sun and the freezing cold of space. None of the other planets in our solar system have air. Without air, life on Earth could not exist.

Over the last few hundred years, we have begun to change the Earth's air. Our cars, trucks, aircraft, and factories give off chemicals and smoke that make the air very dirty. This is known as air pollution.

Air pollution kills plants and animals. It affects the weather, too. If we do not stop the pollution, we could damage our world forever.

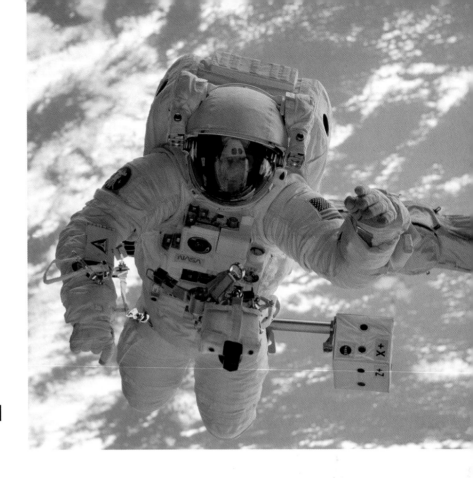

If the Earth was the size of an orange, the layer of air around it would be thinner than the orange peel. When astronauts go into space, they leave Earth's air behind and must take all their oxygen with them.

How fish breathe

Oxygen does not exist only in air. There is oxygen in water, too, but we cannot breathe it in. Fish breathe through gills that separate oxygen from the water. When fish are taken out of water, they "drown" in air.

Fast or slow

Most of the time, you breathe in and out without thinking—your body just does it automatically. But you can make yourself breathe more quickly or slowly when you need to.

When you are sitting quietly, you breathe in and out about 12 to 15 times a minute. This gives you enough energy to keep your body working and to stay warm. When you run around, your muscles need more energy. This means that your body has to take in more oxygen, more quickly. To get that oxygen, your breathing speeds up and you breathe more deeply. Your lungs take in more air and your heart beats faster to pump the extra oxygen quickly around your body.

If you breathe too slowly or shallowly, too much carbon dioxide can build up in your lungs and blood. When this happens, your body makes you open your mouth wide and take a big breath—you are yawning.

If you run fast for a long time, you cannot always get the oxygen you need into your body quickly enough and you "run out of breath." This is your body's way of telling you to slow down or stop, so that it has a chance to replace the oxygen you have used up.

Sometimes when you run or do other exercise, you get a pain in your side called a "cramp." This happens when the diaphragm, the band of muscle under your lungs, does not have enough oxygen. When you stop and breathe deeply for a while, the cramp goes away.

People who run long distances need to train their bodies so they do not run out of breath.

See for yourself

Speeding up

Jump up and down in place for a while. Put one hand on your chest. Can you feel your heart beating? Stop jumping and count how many breaths you take in a minute. You will probably find that you are breathing at least twice as fast as before.

Making noises

Your breath does not only bring oxygen into your body, it also has another use. You use your breath to talk, sing, giggle, and shout.

Sounds come from your throat, from a part of your body called the voice box. The voice box is found at the top of your windpipe, just under your chin. Inside the voice box are two folds of skin—the vocal cords. When you are quiet, the vocal cords are relaxed and there is a big gap between them. Your breath passes through this gap on its way into and out of the windpipe.

Another way of making sounds is to use your breath to blow into a musical instrument.

When you want to talk, muscles in your throat pull the vocal cords together, leaving just a small gap between them. When air is squeezed through this small gap, it makes a sound. It is much easier to make sounds when you are breathing out than when you are breathing in.

You shape sounds into words by moving your tongue, teeth, lips, and the rest of your mouth. Try talking without moving any part of your mouth! To make a loud or a long sound, you need to take a big breath in, so that you have lots of air to let out.

Sounds are made inside the voice box at the top of your windpipe.

Long distance singers

Some whales live so far apart in the ocean that they need to talk to each other across great distances. The singing sounds they make can travel for hundreds of miles under water.

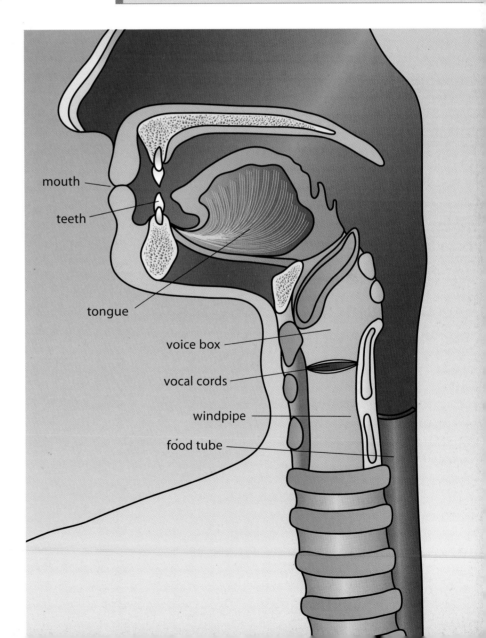

mouth

teeth

tongue

voice box

vocal cords

windpipe

food tube

Coughs and sneezes

If something tickles or irritates your nose or your windpipe, you let out an explosive rush of air to try to clear it. This is a sneeze or a cough.

Air has tiny pieces of dust, dirt, and germs in it. The hairs on the inside of your nose and windpipe work like filters to trap pieces of dirt and stop them from getting into your lungs. Your nose, throat, and windpipe are also lined with a sticky liquid, called mucus. Dust and germs stick to mucus in the same way that flies stick to flypaper.

Hairs in your nose and windpipe trap dirt and dust, and stop them from getting into your lungs.

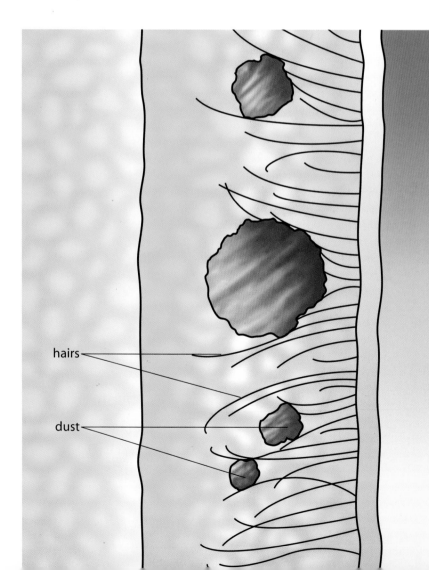

hairs

dust

24

If too much mucus or dust builds up in your nose, your body tries to clear it. You take in a big breath, and the muscles in your throat tighten to hold in the air. Then your stomach muscles squeeze hard and the air is blasted out of your nose in a sneeze, taking the mucus or dust with it.

A cough is the same as a sneeze, except the air is blown out of your mouth instead of your nose. You usually cough to clear mucus or other blockages from your windpipe or throat. The air that is forced out of your mouth or nose also speeds through your voice box, which is why coughs and sneezes are so noisy.

Holding a hankie or a hand over your mouth or nose when you cough or sneeze stops any germs in your breath from spreading.

Having hiccups

Hiccups happen when the diaphragm below your lungs tightens so sharply it makes you take in a sudden gulp of air. The "hic" sound is made by your vocal cords snapping shut as the air rushes in.

Healthy lungs

Now that you know what your lungs do for you, it is a good idea to think about what you can do to keep them healthy.

One way to keep your lungs healthy is to exercise. When your body works hard, it uses up lots of oxygen. You have to breathe deeply to get the extra oxygen into your body, and your heart has to work hard to pump it around your body. This makes your lungs and your heart stronger so that they work better.

The more you exercise your lungs and heart, the healthier they are. Cycling, swimming, and playing sports are all good ways to exercise.

The other important way to keep your lungs healthy is not to smoke. Smoking is bad for your body in lots of ways, but it is especially bad for your lungs. The hairs and mucus in your nose and windpipe cannot trap all the chemicals in cigarette smoke, and they go straight into your lungs. The chemicals attack the cells that make up the lungs and damage the walls of the alveoli.

Breathing in chemicals or very fine dust of any kind can damage your lungs. People with asthma have to be especially careful. Tiny bits of house dust, fur, plant material called pollen, and fumes from traffic can irritate the bronchioles and other air tubes so badly that they swell up. This makes it very hard to breathe, and people with asthma need medicines to help them breathe.

Dirty air

Polluted air is full of dust and chemicals that are dangerous to our health. Aircraft and cars add a lot of pollution to the air. We can all help to prevent this by using them as little as possible.

Most people with asthma carry a small tube called an inhaler. This sends a puff of medicine straight into their air tubes, which makes it easier for air to flow in and out of the lungs.

Body words

Words shown in italics, *like this*, are a guide to how a particular word sounds.

Alveoli *(al–vee–oh–lie)*
Tiny, hollow balls at the ends of the bronchioles in your lungs. Oxygen passes through the alveoli into your blood vessels, and carbon dioxide passes out of your blood vessels into the alveoli. A single alveoli is called an alveolus.

Blood vessels
The network of tubes that carries your blood to every part of your body.

Bronchi *(bron–key)*
Air tubes that branch out from the windpipe through the lungs. A single bronchi is called a bronchus.

Bronchioles *(bron–kee–oles)*
The narrowest air tubes at the ends of the bronchi in your lungs.

Carbon dioxide
One of the Earth's gases. Humans breathe out carbon dioxide from their lungs. Plants use carbon dioxide to make food.

Cells
Tiny pieces of living material that make up all the parts of your body.

Diaphragm *(dye-uh-fram)*
A thick band of muscle that lies between the lungs and the stomach.

Germs
Invisibly small living things that can make us sick and harm our bodies.

Gills
Fish use gills to separate oxygen from water just as people have lungs to separate oxygen from air.

Glucose
A type of sugar found in many of the foods we eat. Our bodies mix glucose and oxygen together to release the energy stored in glucose.

Microscope
An instrument used for seeing objects that are too small to be seen just with the human eye.

Mucus *(mew–kuss)*
A sticky liquid that lines the inside of your nose, throat, and windpipe.

Oxygen
One of the Earth's gases. We breathe in oxygen to produce energy. Plants give out oxygen through tiny holes in their leaves.

Pollen
A fine, yellowish powder made by flowers.

Vocal cords
The part of your throat that uses air to make sounds. You shape the sounds you make by moving different parts of your mouth and throat.

Voice box
The part of your throat that contains your vocal cords.

Water vapor
Tiny droplets of water that are so small and light they float in air.

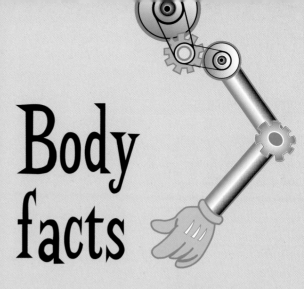

Body facts

- It takes about 6 seconds for blood to travel from the heart to the lungs and back.

- There are up to 300 million alveoli in each of your lungs.

- A bronchiole is only as thick as the hairs on your head.

- Babies breathe very fast— about 25 breaths a minute.

- An adult windpipe is about 5 in. (12 cm) long and $3/4$– $1\,1/5$ in. (2–3 cm) across.

- The air in a sneeze leaves your body at about 100 mph (160 kph).

Index

Web Sites

Due to the changing nature of Internet links, PowerKids Press has developed an online list of Web Sites related to the subject of this book. This site is updated regularly. Please use this link to access this list: www.powerkidslinks.com/body/breathe